RECIPES FROM THE DAIRY

MURDOCH BOOKS

CONTENTS

INTRODUCTION

Since time immemorial, humans have been consuming the products and parts of animals, and among these, milk must surely rank as one of the most important. Throughout much of history, milk provided vital nourishment, including valuable protein, for many communities too poor to afford much, if any, meat.

Animals were first domesticated some 12,000 years ago, so our relationship with sheep, cows and goats goes back a very long way indeed. These days, we invest little to no effort at all in our procurement of milk, cream, cheese and the many other products we loosely term as 'dairy'. A trip to the nearest corner store or supermarket with a bit of spare change easily gets us a carton of milk, some sour cream, a block of cheese or a tub of ricotta. Most sizeable towns and certainly any city will have a specialist deli or a dedicated cheese shop where less mainstream cheesy offerings can be purchased, cut fresh from a wedge or slab.

Over centuries, initially for reasons to do with preserving fresh milk (which is highly perishable), a whole raft of milk-based products has been devised, from the ancient (such as yoghurt and butter) to the modern (such as cream cheese and condensed milk). There is now an enormous range of dairy foods at our disposal.

Milk is a miraculous food. All mammals produce it, but that for human consumption (apart from breast milk for newborns, of course) comes from ruminants. Milk is designed by nature as a sustaining food for infant mammals, and somewhere along the way, humans worked out that it was a highly versatile foodstuff. The principal animals exploited for their milk are cows, sheep, goats, water buffalo (common throughout Asia, parts of the Middle East and in Southern Italy), yak (found in Tibet and Central Asia) and camels (used throughout Northern Africa). Ruminants such as these have a complex digestion that can efficiently process large amounts of feed into copious quantities of milk. The great thing about such animals is that they pose no competition for humans as far as their diet goes, making for a harmonious co-existence.

Until the Industrial Revolution, all dairying was done on a small scale, on farms. People produced as much milk, butter, cheese or yoghurt as they needed, with perhaps a little left over to sell. Supply to urban areas was tricky before refrigeration and it was not uncommon for people (mainly children) to die from drinking contaminated milk. With the advent of the railway in the early to mid-nineteenth century, milk could be regularly and freshly supplied, and improvements in hygiene meant that milk was more reliably 'clean'. Milking machines were invented, and animals no longer served a dual purpose as both workers and milkers. Slowly, a dedicated dairy industry developed.

Now, in the twenty-first century, dairying is (in the developed world, at least) far removed from the traditional image of milk-maids hand-collecting milk in wooden pails from individually named cows. Herds are enormous; cows are bred for their milk-producing efficiency and the entire process of extracting milk and providing it, and other dairy foods, to consumers has become clinical in the extreme, with dairy products now mass produced to a vast extent. As with any food, it is worthwhile to seek out products made in small batches according to artisanal methods, and tasting the difference.

What we have gained in the cheapness of our dairy foods and in the efficiency of their production, we have lost in the richness that comes when natural, slower processes allow for slight and interesting variations in taste and texture. These days there is a growing interest in raw milk and in products made using it; many traditional European cheeses are still made using raw milk and their fans claim them to be far superior in flavour and texture to equivalents made using pasteurised milk.

Of all dairy foods, none provides so much fascination as cheese. The sheer number of cheeses is enormous. The potential for new ones is almost as vast — unique varieties are constantly being developed. Cheese dates back to ancient eras; by the time of the Greeks and Romans, it was an important commodity and was mentioned widely in the literature of the day (including in Homer's *Odyssey*, in which the Cyclops Polyphemus is described making it in his cave). The Roman writer Apicius lists the steps in cheese making when writing in the first century AD.

When all is said and done, cheese is simply a way to preserve milk for later use. Cheese is made by curdling fermented milk, then draining off the liquid that forms (the whey). The curds are generally curdled using rennet, a substance extracted from the stomach of suckling animals, and flavoured with salt. The combination of bacteria used to ferment the milk, in combination with the type of milk and the particular type of cheese-making process employed, plus the action of time as a cheese is matured, are the variables that give rise to the large number of cheeses we know today.

Throughout much of history, cheese has been the food of sophisticates and the humble alike; fresh, simply made cheese was called 'white meat', such was its importance as a protein food on the tables of the poor. The wealthy could afford the more complex cheeses that required skill and long ageing to construct and ripen. By the turn of the last century, the art of cheese making was at its zenith; unfortunately the industrialised processes that then brought cheese fairly cheaply to more tables ultimately led to its standardisation.

Many cheeses are ideal for using in cooking but sometimes there is nothing better than simply savouring a beautifully made specimen, at the peak of ripeness and at room temperature with a few well-chosen accompaniments.

TWICE-BAKED CHEESE SOUFFLES

SERVES 4

250 ml (9 fl oz/1 cup) milk

3 whole black peppercorns

1 onion, cut in half and studded with 2 cloves

1 bay leaf

60 g (2¼ oz) butter

60 g (2¼ oz/½ cup) self-raising flour

2 eggs, separated

125 g (4½ oz/1 cup) grated gruyère cheese

250 ml (9 fl oz/1 cup) cream

50 g (1¾ oz/½ cup) finely grated
   parmesan cheese

METHOD Preheat the oven to 180°C (350°F/Gas 4). Lightly grease four 125 ml (4 fl oz/½ cup) ramekins.

Place the milk, peppercorns, onion and bay leaf in a saucepan and heat until nearly boiling. Remove the saucepan from the heat and let the milk infuse for 10 minutes. Strain, discarding the solids.

Melt the butter in a saucepan over medium heat, add the flour and cook for 1 minute. Stirring constantly, add the milk a little at a time, returning the mixture to a simmer between additions and stirring well to prevent lumps from forming. Simmer the mixture, stirring, until it boils and thickens.

Transfer the mixture to a bowl, add the egg yolks and gruyère cheese and stir to combine well.

Using electric beaters, whisk the egg whites until soft peaks form, then gently fold into the cheese sauce. Divide the mixture among the ramekins and place in a baking dish half-filled with hot water. Bake for 15 minutes. Remove from the baking dish, cool and refrigerate until needed.

Preheat the oven to 200°C (400°F/Gas 6), remove the soufflés from the ramekins and place them onto ovenproof plates. Pour the cream over the top and sprinkle with the parmesan. Bake for 20 minutes, or until puffed and golden. Serve immediately.

MARINATED YOGHURT CHEESE BALLS

MAKES 18

1.5 kg (3 lb/5 oz) Greek-style yoghurt
2 x 50 cm (20 inch) squares muslin
2 fresh bay leaves
3 sprigs thyme
2 sprigs oregano
500 ml (17 fl oz /2 cups) extra virgin olive oil

METHOD Place the yoghurt in a large bowl with 2 teaspoons salt and mix well. Put the muslin squares one on top of the other. Place the yoghurt mixture in the centre. Gather up the corners of the muslin and tie securely with kitchen string, then tie the muslin bag securely to a wooden spoon or similar, and suspend over a bowl. Refrigerate and leave to drain for 3 days, or until the yoghurt is the consistency of ricotta cheese.

Remove the yoghurt from the cloth and place in a bowl. Roll tablespoons of the mixture into balls and place on a large tray; there should be 18 balls. Cover and refrigerate for 3 hours, or until firm.

Place the balls in a clean, dry 1 litre (32 fl oz/4 cup) glass jar with the bay leaves, thyme and oregano sprigs. Add enough olive oil to fill the jar and cover the balls, then seal the jar and refrigerate for up to 1 week.

Before serving, drain the cheese balls well and bring them to room temperature.

NOTE Yoghurt cheese balls are traditionally served at breakfast or as an appetiser, with olives, bread, cold meats and tomato.

POACHED EGGS
WITH YOGHURT

SERVES 4

60 g (2¼ oz) butter
1 onion, thinly sliced
250 g (9 oz/1 cup) Greek-style yoghurt
4 large eggs
1 teaspoon hot paprika

METHOD Preheat the oven to 150°C (300°F/Gas 2). Melt 20 g
(¾ oz) of the butter in a heavy-based frying pan, add the onion
then cook over low heat, stirring often, for 15 minutes, or until
golden. Remove from the pan and cool slightly. Combine the
onion and yoghurt in a bowl, then season to taste with salt.

Divide the yoghurt mixture among four deep 7.5 cm (3 inch)
diameter ovenproof ramekins, then place on a tray in the oven
to heat gently.

Meanwhile, fill a large, deep frying pan three-quarters full with
water, add a pinch of salt and bring to a gentle simmer. Crack an
egg into a saucer, then slide the egg into the simmering water.

Poach for 3 minutes, then remove carefully with a slotted spoon and pat off any excess water with paper towels. Poach all the eggs in the same way. Place an egg in each ramekin and season with salt and pepper.

Melt the remaining butter in a small saucepan and add the paprika. Drizzle over the eggs and serve at once.

BAKED RICOTTA
WITH RATATOUILLE

SERVES 8–10

1.5 kg (3 lb 5 oz) firm ricotta cheese, well drained
(see Note)

4 eggs, lightly beaten

3 garlic cloves, finely chopped

2 tablespoons chopped oregano

sea salt

80 ml (2½ fl oz/⅓ cup) extra virgin olive oil

300 g (10½ oz) eggplant (aubergine), cut into
1.5 cm (⅝ inch) pieces

3 capsicums (peppers) (a mixture of yellow, green
and red), trimmed, seeded and cut into 1.5 cm
(⅝ inch) pieces

400 g (14 oz) tin crushed tomatoes

METHOD Preheat the oven to 180°C (350°F/Gas 4) and lightly
grease a 22 cm (8½ inch) springform cake tin. Combine the
ricotta, eggs, 1 finely chopped garlic clove and 1 tablespoon of
the chopped oregano in a bowl and season to taste with sea salt
and freshly ground black pepper. Pour the ricotta mixture into

the tin, then tap the tin twice on a work surface to expel any air bubbles. Bake the ricotta for 1 hour 30 minutes, or until firm and light golden. Cool the ricotta in the pan on a wire rack, pressing down on the ricotta occasionally to remove any air bubbles.

Meanwhile, heat 2 tablespoons of the oil in a frying pan, add the eggplant and cook for 4–5 minutes, or until golden. Add the capsicum pieces and remaining garlic and cook for 5 minutes, until the capsicum softens, adding an extra tablespoon of oil, if necessary. Stir in the tomato and remaining oregano and cook for 10–15 minutes, or until the mixture is reduced slightly and the vegetables are tender. Season to taste with sea salt and freshly ground black pepper.

Remove the ricotta from the pan and cut into wedges. Serve the ricotta wedges with some ratatouille on the side.

NOTE Buy ricotta in bulk from a delicatessen or cheese shop; it has a better texture and fresher flavour than the bland, paste-like ricotta sold in tubs in supermarkets.

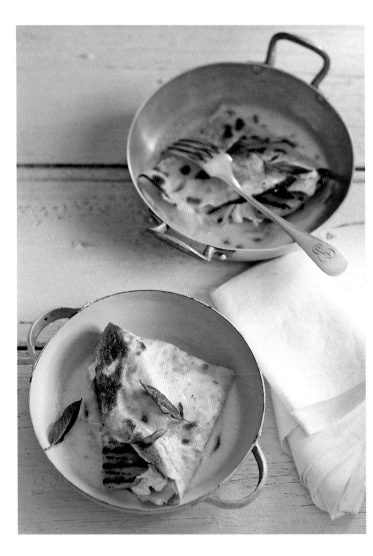

GRATIN OF CREPES WITH PUMPKIN, GOAT'S CHEESE & CRISP SAGE LEAVES

SERVE 6

CREPE BATTER
310 ml (10³/₄ fl oz/1¹/₄ cups) milk
50 g (1³/₄ oz) butter, chopped, plus extra for pan-frying
155 g (5¹/₂ oz/1¹/₄ cups) plain (all-purpose) flour
3 eggs

FILLING
400 g (14 oz) butternut pumpkin (squash), peeled
2 tablespoons olive oil
125 ml (4 fl oz/¹/₂ cup) vegetable oil
30 g (1 oz) sage leaves
250 g (9 oz/2 cups) crumbled soft goat's cheese

TOPPING
300 ml (10¹/₂ fl oz) cream
150 g (5¹/₂ oz) fontina cheese, grated

METHOD   To make the crepe batter, gently heat the milk and butter in a small saucepan until the butter has melted; do not allow the milk to boil. Combine the flour and a pinch of salt in a large bowl and make a well in the centre. Add the eggs to the well and slowly whisk in the warm milk mixture. Whisk until completely smooth — the mixture will be quite thin. Cover and stand for 10–15 minutes.

Heat a nonstick frying pan over medium heat, then melt a little butter over the base of the pan. Add 60 ml (2 fl oz/¼ cup) of the crepe batter to the pan and swirl to cover the base. Cook for 30 seconds, or until the crepe is set and bubbles start to appear on the surface. Using a spatula, carefully turn the crepe over and cook for another 30 seconds. Transfer to a plate.

Repeat with the remaining batter until you have 12 perfect crepes. (There is enough batter to allow for a few practice ones as well.)

Heat a chargrill pan over medium heat. Cut the pumpkin into 24 slices, each about 1 cm (½ inch) thick. Put the pumpkin in a large bowl with the olive oil and ground pepper and toss to coat. Chargrill the pumpkin in batches for about 2 minutes, or until cooked through, turning once. Cool.

Heat the vegetable oil in a small frying pan until the oil creates a haze; take care that it does not burn. Add the sage leaves to the pan, in batches, cook until crisp, then remove and drain on paper towels.

Preheat the grill (broiler) to high. Place 2 pumpkin slices, some goat's cheese and a few sage leaves over one quarter of each crepe, saving some sage leaves to garnish. Fold each crepe in half, then in half again, to form neat triangles. Divide the crepes among four ovenproof gratin dishes or shallow pasta dishes.

To make the topping, heat the cream in a small saucepan, then stir in the grated cheese. Pour the mixture evenly over the crepes. Sit the dishes on a large baking tray, put the tray under the grill and cook for 3–5 minutes, or until the cheese is bubbling and hot. Scatter with the reserved crisp sage leaves and serve.

ASPARAGUS, PECORINO & MINT FRITTATA

SERVES 4

6 eggs
120 g (4 1/2 oz/1 1/3 cups) grated pecorino cheese
1 large handful mint, finely shredded
200 g (7 oz) baby asparagus spears, trimmed
2 tablespoons extra virgin oil

METHOD Put the eggs in a bowl, whisk well, then stir in the
cheese and mint. Preheat the oven grill (broiler) to medium–high.

Cut the asparagus into short pieces. Heat the oil in a 20 cm
(8 inch) frying pan. Add the asparagus and cook for 4–5 minutes,
stirring often, until tender and bright green. Season to taste, then
reduce the heat to low. Pour the egg mixture over the asparagus
and cook for 8–10 minutes, using a spatula to gently pull the
sides of the frittata away from the sides of the pan and tipping
the pan slightly so the egg runs underneath the cooked base.

When the mixture is nearly set, place the pan under the grill for
1–2 minutes, until the top is set and just browned. Serve warm.

GNOCCHI ROMANA

SERVES 4

750 ml (26 fl oz/4 cups) milk
a pinch of ground nutmeg
200 g (7 oz/1²/₃ cups) fine semolina
3 egg yolks
65 g (2¹/₄ oz/²/₃ cup) grated parmesan cheese
30 g (1 oz) butter, melted
80 ml (2¹/₂ fl oz/¹/₃ cup) cream
75 g (2¹/₂ oz/¹/₂ cup) grated mozzarella cheese

METHOD   Line a deep swiss roll (jelly roll) tin with baking
paper. In a saucepan, combine the milk, nutmeg, salt and freshly
ground black pepper to taste. Bring to the boil, reduce the heat
and gradually stir in the semolina. Cook, stirring frequently, for
5–10 minutes, or until the mixture is very thick.

Remove the pan from the heat and allow to cool slightly. Beat
the egg yolks and half the parmesan cheese together in a small
bowl. Stir into the semolina, then spread the mixture in the
prepared tin. Cool slightly, then refrigerate for 1 hour, or until
the mixture is firm.

Preheat the oven to 180°C (350°F/Gas 4). Using a floured 4 cm (1½ inch) biscuit (cookie) cutter, cut the semolina into rounds and arrange them in a greased shallow overproof dish. Pour the butter and cream over the semolina, then sprinkle with the combined mozzarella and remaining parmesan.

Bake for 20–25 minutes, or until the gnocchi are golden and bubbling and heated through. Season with freshly ground black pepper and serve.

BAKED PRAWNS WITH FETA

SERVES 4 AS A FIRST COURSE

300 g (10 oz) raw large prawns (shrimp)
2 tablespoons olive oil
2 small red onions, finely chopped
1 large garlic clove, crushed
350 g (12 oz) ripe tomatoes, diced
2 tablespoons lemon juice
2 tablespoons oregano, or 1 teaspoon dried oregano
120 g (4¼ oz) feta cheese
extra virgin olive oil, for drizzling
chopped flat-leaf (Italian) parsley, to garnish

METHOD Preheat the oven to 180°C (350°F/Gas 4).

Peel the prawns, leaving the tails intact. Working from the head end, gently pull out and discard the intestinal tract (the dark vein) from each prawn tail.

Heat the olive oil in a saucepan over medium heat, add the red onion and cook, stirring occasionally, for 3 minutes, or until softened. Add the crushed garlic and cook for a few seconds, then add the tomato and cook for 10 minutes, or until the mixture is slightly reduced and thickened. Add the lemon juice and oregano, then season to taste.

Spoon the hot sauce into a shallow baking dish, about 15 cm (6 inches) square. Place the prawns on top. Crumble the feta over the prawns, then drizzle with oil and sprinkle with freshly ground black pepper.

Bake for 15 minutes, or until the prawns are just cooked. Sprinkle with the parsley and serve immediately.

EGGPLANT SALAD WITH GARLIC–YOGHURT DRESSING

SERVES 6

1 kg (2 lb 4 oz) large eggplants (aubergines)
125 ml (4 fl oz/1/2 cup) olive oil
1 onion, finely chopped
1/2 teaspoon ground cinnamon
4 garlic cloves, crushed
2 x 400 g (14 oz) tins crushed tomatoes
2 tablespoons chopped coriander (cilantro)
3 tablespoons chopped flat-leaf (Italian) parsley
1 tablespoon lemon juice
2 tablespoons chopped mint
150 g (51/2 oz/2/3 cup) Greek-style
   natural yoghurt
25 g (1 oz) toasted pine nuts
toasted country-style bread, to serve

METHOD Cut the eggplants into 2 cm (3/4 inch) pieces, place in a colander over a bowl and sprinkle generously with salt. Leave for 30 minutes, rinse under cold water, then pat dry with a tea towel (dish towel).

Heat 2 tablespoons olive oil in a large frying pan and fry the eggplant, in batches, until golden, adding more oil if necessary. Drain well on paper towels.

Heat another 2 tablespoons oil in the pan, add the onion then cook, stirring often, over medium heat for 1 minute. Add the cinnamon and half the garlic, cook for 1 minute, then add the tomatoes. Add the eggplant, bring the mixture to a simmer, then cook over medium–low heat for 1 hour, or until the mixture is quite dry. Add half of both the coriander and parsley. Stir and leave to cool.

Mix 2 tablespoons olive oil with the lemon juice. Add the remaining garlic and all the mint, then stir into the yoghurt.

Gently toss the pine nuts and remaining fresh herbs through the salad. Serve at room temperature with the toast and dressing.

BEETROOT & BLUE CHEESE SALAD

SERVES 4

1 tablespoon olive oil

50 g (1 3/4 oz/1/2 cup) pecans

1.3 kg (3 lb) small beetroot (beets), washed, trimmed and halved

250 g (9 oz) baby green beans, trimmed

120 g (4 1/4 oz/4 cups) watercress, trimmed

2 tablespoons walnut oil

1 teaspoon honey

2 teaspoons finely grated orange zest

1 tablespoon cider vinegar

50 g (1 3/4 oz) firm blue cheese, such as stilton, crumbled

METHOD Heat the olive oil in a frying pan over medium–high heat, then add the pecans. Cook, stirring often, for 3 minutes, or until the pecans are lightly toasted, then sprinkle with salt and freshly ground black pepper. Remove the pan from the heat and pour the pecans into a bowl lined with paper towels. Set aside to drain.

Line a large steamer with baking paper, punch holes in the paper, then place the beetroot in the steamer and cover with a lid. Set the steamer over a saucepan of boiling water and cook the beetroot for 30–35 minutes, or until tender when pierced with a knife. Remove from the steamer and cool, reserving the water in the saucepan.

Remove the baking paper from the steamer, add the beans to the steamer, cover and cook for 5–7 minutes, or until just tender. Remove the beans and refresh under cold water.

Peel the beetroot, trim off any excess stem and cut into wedges or chunks. Combine the pecans, beans and watercress in a large bowl. Whisk together the walnut oil, honey, orange zest and vinegar in a bowl, then pour over the salad. Add the beetroot and stir gently to just combine. Season to taste, then transfer to a serving platter and sprinkle the blue cheese over to serve.

ZUCCHINI & HALOUMI FRITTERS

MAKES 36; SERVES 6

300 g (10¹/2 oz) zucchini (courgettes)
4 spring onions (scallions), thinly sliced
200 g (7 oz) haloumi cheese, coarsely grated
30 g (1 oz/¹/4 cup) plain (all-purpose) flour
2 eggs
1 tablespoon chopped dill, plus extra sprigs, to garnish
60 ml (2 fl oz/¹/4 cup) vegetable oil
1 lemon, cut into thin wedges
90 g (3¹/4 oz/¹/3 cup) Greek-style yoghurt

METHOD Preheat the oven to 120°C (235°F/Gas ¹/2). Coarsely grate the zucchini, then squeeze out the liquid. Combine with the spring onion, haloumi, flour, eggs and dill. Season well.

Heat the oil in a large heavy-based frying pan. Drop heaped teaspoons of mixture into the pan and cook for 2 minutes each side, or until golden. Drain on paper towels, then transfer to the oven to keep warm while cooking the remaining fritters. Serve the fritters with yoghurt, a piece of lemon and a sprig of dill.

LAMB KEBABS WITH MINT BUTTERMILK SAUCE

SERVES 4

5 garlic cloves, chopped
5 cm (2 inch) piece ginger, chopped
3 green chillies, chopped
1 onion, chopped
3 tablespoons Greek-style yoghurt
3 tablespoons coriander (cilantro) leaves
500 g (1 lb 2 oz) minced (ground) lamb
red onion rings and lemon wedges, to serve

MINT BUTTERMILK SAUCE
1 teaspoon cumin seeds
1/2 cup mint leaves, chopped
1/2 cup coriander (cilantro), chopped
2 cm (3/4 inch) piece ginger, chopped
2 green chillies, chopped
310 ml (10 3/4 fl oz/1 1/4 cups) Greek-style yoghurt
310 ml (10 3/4 fl oz/1 1/4 cups) buttermilk

METHOD   Combine the garlic, ginger, chilli, onion, yoghurt and coriander leaves in a food processor and process until a thick, smooth paste forms. Season with salt and freshly ground black pepper, then combine with the lamb in a bowl and mix well. Divide the mixture into 16 even-sized pieces, then shape into oval patties and cover and chill for 20 minutes.

Meanwhile, make the mint buttermilk sauce. Place a small, heavy-based frying pan over low heat, add the cumin seeds, then dry-fry, shaking the pan, for 2 minutes or until aromatic. Cool, then grind the seeds to a fine powder using an electric spice grinder or a mortar and pestle.

Combine the mint leaves, coriander, ginger and chilli in a food processor or blender, then process or blend until the mixture forms a smooth paste. Add the yoghurt and buttermilk to the mixture in the food processor then process until well combined and smooth. Season to taste with sea salt and freshly ground black pepper, then stir in the cumin.

Preheat the grill (broiler) to high. Thread four meatballs onto each of four metal skewers then grill (broil) for about 7 minutes, or until brown. Turn and cook the other side for 6–7 minutes, or until the meatballs are browned and cooked through. Serve with the mint buttermilk sauce, red onion rings and lemon wedges.

OPEN LASAGNE WITH ROCKET & WALNUT PESTO

SERVES 4

PESTO

100 g (3 1/2 oz/1 cup) walnuts

2 garlic cloves

2 large handfuls baby rocket (arugula)

1 large handful basil

1 large handful flat-leaf (Italian) parsley

100 ml (3 1/2 fl oz) extra virgin olive oil

80 ml (2 1/2 fl oz/1/3 cup) walnut oil

50 g (1 3/4 oz/1/2 cup) grated pecorino cheese

100 g (3 1/2 oz/1 cup) grated parmesan cheese

375 g (13 oz) fresh lasagne sheets

1 tablespoon olive oil

100 g (3 1/2 oz/2 cups) baby English spinach

1 garlic clove, sliced

2 tablespoons lemon juice

200 g (7 oz/1 2/3 cups) crumbled marinated goat's
   feta cheese

2 tablespoons finely grated parmesan cheese

METHOD   To make the pesto, preheat the oven to 180°C (350°F/Gas 4). Rinse the walnuts in cold water, shake dry, spread on a baking tray and bake for 5–8 minutes, or until light golden. Transfer the toasted walnuts to a food processor and add the garlic, rocket, basil and parsley. Using the pulse button, process the mixture just until it resembles coarse breadcrumbs. With the motor running, add the oils in a thin, steady stream, then add the pecorino and parmesan cheeses and process for 40 seconds. Transfer the pesto to a bowl and cover with plastic wrap.

Cut the lasagne sheets into sixteen 8 cm (3¼ inch) squares. Cook a few squares at a time in a large saucepan of boiling salted water for 4 minutes, or until al dente. Lay them on a clean tea towel (dish towel) and cover to keep warm.

Heat the olive oil in a large frying pan over medium heat, add the spinach and garlic and sauté until just wilted. Stir in the lemon juice, cover and keep warm.

Spoon 1 tablespoon of the pesto onto four plates and spread out to the size of the pasta squares. Cover with a pasta square, then divide one-third of the spinach among the pasta squares. Sprinkle with one-third of the goat's feta, cover with another pasta square and spread with pesto. Repeat the layers, finishing with pesto. Sprinkle with the grated parmesan and serve immediately.

GOAT'S CHEESE GALETTE

SERVES 6

PASTRY
125 g (4 1/2 oz/1 cup) plain (all-purpose) flour
60 ml (2 fl oz/1/4 cup) olive oil

FILLING
1 tablespoon olive oil
2 onions, thinly sliced
1 teaspoon thyme leaves
125 g (4 1/2 oz/1/2 cup) firm ricotta cheese (see Note)
100 g (3 1/2 oz/3/4 cup) crumbled soft goat's cheese
2 tablespoons pitted black olives
1 egg, lightly beaten
60 ml (2 fl oz/1/4 cup) cream

METHOD For the pastry, sift the flour and a pinch of salt into a large bowl and make a well in the centre. Add the olive oil and mix with a flat-bladed knife until crumbly. Gradually add 3–4 tablespoons chilled water and mix until a coarse dough forms. Transfer to a lightly floured surface and form into a disc. Wrap in plastic wrap and refrigerate for 30 minutes.

For the filling, heat the oil in a frying pan, add the onion, cover and cook over low heat, stirring occasionally, for 30 minutes. Season to taste with sea salt and freshly ground black pepper, then stir in half the thyme. Cool slightly.

Preheat the oven to 180°C (350°F/Gas 4). Roll out the pastry on a sheet of baking paper to a 30 cm (12 inch) circle. Transfer the baking paper and pastry to a baking tray. Evenly spread the onion over the pastry, leaving a 3 cm (1¼ inch) border. Sprinkle the ricotta and the goat's cheese evenly over the onion. Place the olives over the cheeses, then sprinkle with the remaining thyme. Fold the pastry border in to the edge of the filling, gently pleating as you go.

Combine the egg and cream in a bowl, then carefully pour over the filling. Bake in the lower half of the oven for 45 minutes, or until the pastry is golden. Serve warm or at room temperature.

NOTE Buy ricotta in bulk from a delicatessen or cheese shop; it has a better texture and fresher flavour than the bland, paste-like ricotta sold in tubs in supermarkets.

FILLED CHEESE BISCUITS

SERVES 4–6

BISCUIT PASTRY

125 g (4 1/2 oz/1 cup) plain (all-purpose) flour
1/2 teaspoon baking powder
60 g (2 1/2 oz) cold butter, chopped
1 egg, lightly beaten
60 g (2 1/4 oz) grated cheddar cheese
1 teaspoon finely snipped chives
1 teaspoon finely chopped marjoram
1 tablespoon iced water

CHEESE FILLING

80 g (2 3/4 oz) cream cheese, at room temperature
20 g (3/4 oz) butter, softened
1 tablespoon finely snipped chives
1 tablespoon finely chopped flat-leaf (Italian) parsley
1/2 teaspoon finely grated lemon zest
90 g (3 1/4 oz/3/4 cup) finely grated cheddar cheese

METHOD Preheat the oven to 190°C (375°F/Gas 5). Line two
baking trays with baking paper.

To make the biscuit pastry, sift the flour and baking powder into a large bowl, then add the chopped butter. Using your fingertips, rub in the butter until the mixture resembles fine breadcrumbs. Make a well in the centre, add the egg, cheese, herbs and iced water to the well and mix with a flat-bladed knife until a coarse dough forms. Transfer the mixture to a lightly floured surface and gather into a ball.

Roll out the pastry between two sheets of baking paper until 3 mm (1/8 inch) thick. Remove the top sheet and cut the pastry into rounds, using a 5 cm (2 inch) cutter. Place the rounds on the baking trays. Re-roll pastry scraps and cut out more rounds. Bake the biscuits for 8 minutes, or until light brown. Transfer to a wire rack to cool.

To make the filling, using electric beaters, beat the cream cheese and butter in a small bowl until light and creamy. Add the herbs, lemon zest and cheese, season to taste with freshly ground black pepper and beat until smooth. Spread 1/2 teaspoon of the filling on half the biscuits and sandwich with the remaining biscuits.

Unfilled biscuits will keep, stored in an airtight container in a cool, dark place, for 2 days. Filled biscuits are best served on the day of filling.

STILTON SOUP

SERVES 4–6

30 g (1 oz) butter
2 leeks, white part only, chopped
1 kg (2 lb 4 oz) potatoes, chopped into chunks
1.25 litres (44 fl oz/5 cups) chicken stock
125 ml (4 fl oz/½ cup) cream
100 g (3½ oz) stilton cheese
thyme sprigs, to garnish

METHOD Melt the butter in a large saucepan, add the leek and cook, stirring often, over medium heat for 6–7 minutes, or until softened. Add the potato and stock and bring to the boil, then simmer, covered, for 15 minutes, or until the potato is tender.

Transfer the mixture to a blender or food processor and blend or process until smooth.

Return the mixture to the saucepan, add the cream and cheese, then stir over low heat until the cheese has melted; do not allow the mixture to boil. Divide the soup among warmed bowls, garnish with sprigs of thyme and serve immediately.

MUSHROOM PIROSHKI

MAKES 20

310 g (11 oz/2^1/$_2$ cups) plain (all-purpose) flour
180 g (6^1/$_4$ oz) cold butter, chopped
1 egg yolk
60 g (2^1/$_4$ oz/^{1}/$_4$ cup) sour cream

FILLING
150 g (5^1/$_2$ oz) Swiss brown mushrooms, wiped
   clean and coarsely chopped
50 g (1^3/$_4$ oz) butter
1 small onion, finely chopped
95 g (3^1/$_4$ oz/^{1}/$_2$ cup) cooked short-grain rice
1 hard-boiled egg, finely chopped
2 tablespoons chopped flat-leaf (Italian) parsley
2 tablespoons finely chopped dill
1 egg, lightly beaten

METHOD Sift the flour and ^{1}/$_2$ teaspoon salt into a large bowl
and add the chopped butter. Using your fingertips, rub in the
butter until the mixture resembles fine breadcrumbs. Add the
combined egg yolk and sour cream then, using a flat-bladed

knife, mix until a coarse dough forms, adding a little iced water, if necessary. Turn the dough out onto a lightly floured surface and press together into a smooth ball. Wrap in plastic wrap and refrigerate for 30 minutes.

To make the filling, process the mushrooms in a food processor until finely chopped. Melt the butter in a frying pan, add the chopped onion and cook, stirring often, for 3–4 minutes, or until softened. Add the chopped mushrooms and cook, stirring, for another 3 minutes, then stir in the rice. Transfer the mixture to a bowl and cool. Stir in the chopped eggs and herbs and season to taste with sea salt and freshly ground black pepper.

Cut the pastry in half, then roll each piece out thickly on a lightly floured surface. Using an 8 cm (3¼ inch) plain biscuit (cookie) cutter, cut 10 rounds from each piece of dough. Place 1 tablespoon of filling in the centre of each round. Brush the edge of each round with a little beaten egg then fold over to form a half-moon shape, pinching the edges together to seal. Prick the tops of the pastries several times with a fork, then transfer to a baking tray and refrigerate for 30 minutes.

Preheat the oven the 190°C (375°F/Gas 5). Brush the pastries with beaten egg, then bake for 15 minutes, or until golden. Serve hot.

BORLOTTI BEAN MOUSSAKA

SERVES 6

250 g (9 oz/1 1/4 cups) dried borlotti beans

2 large eggplants (aubergines)

80 ml (2 1/2 fl oz/1/3 cup) olive oil

1 onion, chopped

1 garlic clove, crushed

125 g (4 1/2 oz) button mushrooms,
    wiped clean and sliced

250 ml (9 fl oz/1 cup) red wine

2 x 440 g (15 1/2 oz) tins diced, peeled tomatoes

1 tablespoon tomato paste (concentrated purée)

1 tablespoon chopped oregano

TOPPING

250 g (9 oz/1 cup) plain yoghurt

4 eggs, lightly beaten

500 ml (17 fl oz/ 2 cups) milk

1/4 teaspoon sweet paprika

50 g (1 3/4 oz/1/2 cup) grated parmesan cheese

40 g (1 1/2 oz/1/2 cup) fresh breadcrumbs

METHOD Soak the beans in cold water overnight. Drain well and rinse. Transfer to a saucepan, cover with water and bring to the boil. Reduce the heat to a simmer and cook for 1½ hours, or until tender. Drain well and spoon into a large ovenproof dish.

Meanwhile, preheat the oven grill (broiler) to medium–high. Slice the eggplant, sprinkle with salt and set aside for 30 minutes. Rinse the eggplant, then pat dry on paper towels. Brush all over with oil, then grill for 3 minutes on each side, or until golden. Drain the eggplant on paper towels. Preheat the oven to 200°C (400°F/Gas 6).

Heat the remaining olive oil in a large, heavy-based saucepan. Add the onion and garlic and cook over medium heat for 4–5 minutes, or until the onion is golden. Add the mushrooms and cook for 3 minutes, or until browned. Add the wine and cook over high heat for 2–3 minutes. Stir in the tomatoes, tomato paste and oregano and bring to the boil. Reduce the heat and simmer for 40 minutes, or until thickened. Spoon the sauce over the borlotti beans and top with the eggplant slices.

To make the topping, whisk together the yoghurt, eggs, milk and paprika, then pour over the eggplant. Allow to stand for 10 minutes. Combine the parmesan and breadcrumbs then sprinkle over the top. Bake for 50–55 minutes, or until golden.

SPAGHETTI CARBONARA

SERVES 6

500 g (1 lb 2 oz) dried spaghetti
8 rindless bacon slices (about 450 g/1 lb)
2 teaspoons olive oil
4 eggs, lightly beaten
50 g (1 $^3/_4$ oz/$^1/_2$ cup) freshly grated parmesan cheese
300 ml (10 $^1/_2$ fl oz/1 $^1/_4$ cups) cream

METHOD Cook the spaghetti in a large saucepan of boiling salted water until al dente, then drain and return to the pan.

Meanwhile, cut the bacon into strips. Heat the oil in a heavy-based frying pan, add the bacon and cook over medium heat, stirring, for 5 minutes, or until crisp. Drain on paper towels.

Working quickly, whisk the eggs, parmesan and cream in a bowl until combined. Add the bacon, then pour over the hot pasta. Toss to coat the pasta with the sauce and stir over very low heat for 1 minute, or until slightly thickened — do not overheat the sauce, or the eggs will scramble. Season with freshly ground black pepper, then divide among warm bowls.

VEAL PARMIGIANA

SERVES 4

4 thin veal steaks
100 g (3 1/2 oz/1 cup) dry breadcrumbs
1/2 teaspoon dried basil
25 g (3/4 oz/1/4 cup) finely grated parmesan cheese,
    plus 50 g (1 3/4 oz/1/2 cup) extra
plain (all-purpose) flour, for coating
1 egg, lightly beaten
1 tablespoon milk
olive oil, for frying
250 g (9 oz/1 cup) tomato passata (puréed tomatoes)
100 g (3 1/2 oz/2/3 cup) grated mozzarella cheese

METHOD Trim the meat of any excess fat and sinew, place between two sheets of plastic wrap and gently pound with a meat mallet until 5 mm (1/4 inch) thick. Snip the edges to prevent the meat from curling while cooking.

Combine the breadcrumbs, basil and parmesan on a sheet of baking paper. Dust the veal steaks in flour, shaking off any excess. Working with one at a time, dip the steaks into the combined egg and milk, allowing any excess to drip off. Coat with the breadcrumb mixture, lightly shaking off the excess. Refrigerate for 30 minutes to firm the coating.

Preheat the oven to 180°C (350°F/ Gas 4). Heat the olive oil in a frying pan and brown the veal steaks over medium heat for 2 minutes on each side, working in batches, if necessary. Drain on paper towels.

Spread half the tomato passata into a shallow ovenproof dish. Arrange the veal steaks on top in a single layer and spoon over the remaining sauce. Top with the extra parmesan and the mozzarella and bake for 20 minutes, or until the cheeses are melted and golden brown. Serve immediately.

ARTICHOKE & PROVOLONE QUICHES

MAKES 6

250 g (9 oz/2 cups) plain (all-purpose) flour
125 g (4 1/2 oz) butter, cut into cubes
1 egg yolk
about 3 tablespoons iced water

FILLING
6 eggs, lightly beaten
3 teaspoons wholegrain mustard
200 g (7 oz/1 1/2 cups) grated provolone piccante cheese
300 g (10 1/2 oz) marinated artichokes, sliced
125 g (4 1/2 oz/3/4 cup) chopped semi-dried
   (sun-blushed) tomatoes

METHOD To make the pastry, combine the flour and butter in
a bowl then, using your fingertips, rub in the butter until the
mixture resembles breadcrumbs. Make a well in the centre, add
the egg yolk and 3 tablespoons iced water to the well, then stir
with a flat-bladed knife until a coarse dough forms, adding a
little more water if needed.

Turn the dough out onto a floured surface and gather into a ball. Wrap in plastic wrap and refrigerate for at least 30 minutes.

Preheat the oven to 190°C (375°F/Gas 5). Grease six 11 cm (4 1/2 inch) fluted pie tins.

To make the filling, combine the eggs, mustard and grated cheese in a bowl.

Divide the pastry into six even-sized pieces. Roll each out to a circle about 3 mm (1/8 inch) thick and use it to line the prepared tins. Trim the edges of the pastry. Divide the artichokes and tomatoes among the pastry cases, pour the egg mixture over and bake for 25 minutes, or until golden. Serve warm.

LEEK, TALEGGIO & APPLE RISOTTO

SERVES 6

1.25 litres (44 fl oz/5 cups) chicken or vegetable stock
2 tablespoons extra virgin olive oil
2 tablespoons unsalted butter
2 leeks, trimmed and cut into 5 mm (1/4 inch) thick rounds
400 g (14 oz/1 3/4 cups) arborio rice
2 granny smith apples, halved lengthways, cored and
    thinly sliced
250 ml (9 fl oz/1 cup) dry white wine
200 g (7 oz) taleggio cheese, chopped
3–4 sage leaves, finely chopped, plus extra, to garnish

METHOD Heat the stock in a saucepan over medium heat and keep to a gentle simmer.

Heat the oil and butter in a large saucepan, add the leek and cook over medium–low heat for 4–5 minutes, or until softened. Add the rice and apple and cook, stirring, for 2–3 minutes, or until the rice is well coated and heated through. Add the wine and cook, stirring, until the wine is absorbed.

Add the simmering stock to the rice and apple mixture, 250 ml
(8 fl oz/1 cup) at a time, stirring constantly until the stock is
absorbed before adding any more, until the rice is very creamy
and tender.

Remove from the heat, stir in the taleggio and chopped sage
and season to taste with sea salt and freshly ground black
pepper. Divide among warmed bowls, decorate with sage leaves
and serve immediately.

PASSIONFRUIT TART

SERVES 8

135 g (4³/4 oz) plain (all-purpose) flour

3 tablespoons icing (confectioners') sugar

3 tablespoons custard powder or instant vanilla
pudding mix

45 g (1¹/2 oz) butter, cut into cubes

4 tablespoons light evaporated milk

FILLING

125 g (4 oz/¹/2 cup) ricotta cheese (see Note)

1 teaspoon natural vanilla extract

30 g (1 oz/¹/4 cup) icing (confectioners') sugar

2 eggs, lightly beaten

4 tablespoons passionfruit pulp (about 4 passionfruit)

185 ml (6 fl oz/³/4 cup) light evaporated milk

icing (confectioners') sugar, for dusting

METHOD Preheat the oven to 200°C (400°F/ Gas 6). Lightly
grease a 23 cm (8¹/2 inch) loose-based flan (tart) tin. Sift the
flour, icing sugar and custard powder into a bowl and rub in the
butter until crumbs form. Add enough evaporated milk to form

a soft dough. Turn out on a floured surface, bring the dough together, then gather into a ball, wrap in plastic wrap and chill for 15 minutes.

Roll out the pastry on a lightly floured surface to fit the tin, trim the edges, then refrigerate for 15 minutes. Cover with baking paper and fill with baking beads, dried beans or rice. Bake for 10 minutes, then remove the rice or beans and paper and bake for another 5–8 minutes, or until golden. Allow to cool.

Reduce the oven to 160°C (315°F/Gas 2–3).

Beat the ricotta with the vanilla extract and icing sugar until smooth. Add the eggs, passionfruit pulp and evaporated milk, then beat well. Put the tin with the pastry case on a baking tray and pour in the filling. Bake for 40 minutes, or until set. Cool in the tin. Dust with icing sugar to serve.

NOTE Buy ricotta in bulk from a delicatessen or cheese shop; it has a better texture and fresher flavour than the bland, paste-like ricotta sold in tubs in supermarkets.

CAPPUCCINO & CHOCOLATE MUFFINS

MAKES 8

20 g ($^3/_4$ oz/$^1/_4$ cup) instant espresso coffee granules

1 tablespoon boiling water

310 g (11 oz/$2^1/_2$ cups) self-raising flour

115 g (4 oz/$^1/_2$ cup) caster (superfine) sugar

2 eggs, lightly beaten

375 ml (13 fl oz/$1^1/_2$ cups) buttermilk

1 teaspoon natural vanilla extract

150 g ($5^1/_2$ oz) butter, melted

100 g ($3^1/_2$ oz/$^2/_3$ cup) chopped good-quality dark chocolate

30 g (1 oz) butter, extra

3 tablespoons soft brown sugar

METHOD Preheat the oven to 200°C (400°F/Gas 6). Grease the bases of eight 125 ml (4 fl oz/$^1/_2$-cup) capacity ramekins. Cut eight rectangular strips of baking paper 8 x 22 cm ($3^1/_4$ x $8^1/_2$ inches) and roll them into cylinders to fit the ramekins. Secure the cylinders with string and place the ramekins on a baking tray.

Dissolve the coffee in the boiling water, then set aside to cool.
Sift the flour and sugar into a large bowl.

Combine the egg, buttermilk, vanilla, melted butter, chocolate
and the coffee mixture in a bowl and stir to mix well. Add the
buttermilk mixture to the flour mixture then, using a large metal
spoon, quickly stir to just combine.

Divide the mixture among the prepared ramekins. Combine the
extra butter and brown sugar in a small saucepan and stir over
medium heat for 1–2 minutes or until the butter has melted and
the sugar dissolves. Spoon the mixture over the muffins then,
using a skewer, gently swirl into the top of each.

Bake the muffins for 25–30 minutes, or until they are cooked
when tested with a skewer. Allow them to cool slightly in the
ramekins before serving.

POLENTA & SOUR CREAM POUND CAKE

SERVES 10–12

150 g (5^{1}/2 oz) butter
230 g (8^{1}/2 oz/1 cup) soft brown sugar
115 g (4 oz/^{1}/2 cup) caster (superfine) sugar
5 eggs
185 g (6^{1}/2 oz/^{3}/4 cup) sour cream
^{1}/2 teaspoon natural almond extract
1 teaspoon natural vanilla extract
155 g (5^{1}/2 oz/1^{1}/4 cups) plain (all-purpose) flour
1^{1}/2 teaspoons baking powder
150 g (5^{1}/2 oz/1 cup) fine polenta
whipped cream, to serve

BOYSENBERRY COMPOTE
80 g (2^{3}/4 oz/^{1}/3 cup) caster (superfine) sugar
2 teaspoons lemon juice
500 g (1 lb 2 oz/3^{3}/4 cups) boysenberries

METHOD Preheat the oven to 180°C (350°F/Gas 4). Grease a
24 x 14 cm (9^{1}/2 x 5^{1}/2 inch) loaf tin.

Using electric beaters, cream the butter, brown sugar and caster sugar in a large bowl until pale and fluffy. Add the eggs one at a time, beating well after each addition. Reduce the speed to low and mix in the sour cream and almond and vanilla extracts.

Sift together the flour, baking powder and a pinch of salt. Add the flour mixture and polenta to the butter mixture and gently stir to combine well. Spoon into the prepared tin, smooth the surface, then bake for 50 minutes, or until cooked when tested with a skewer. Cool in the tin for 5 minutes, then turn out onto a wire rack to cool completely.

Meanwhile, make the boysenberry compote. Combine the sugar, lemon juice and 2 tablespoons water in a saucepan, then stir over medium heat for 3 minutes, or until the sugar dissolves. Add the berries, stir to coat, and bring the mixture to a simmer. Cook over medium–low heat for 5 minutes, stirring occasionally, or until the berries are soft but still holding their shape. Cool to room temperature before serving, or chill if you prefer.

Cut the pound cake into thick slices and serve toasted with the compote and cream.

PETITS POTS DE CREME

SERVES 4

1 vanilla bean
400 ml (14 fl oz) milk
3 egg yolks
1 egg, lightly beaten
80 g (2³/4 oz/¹/3 cup) caster (superfine) sugar

METHOD Preheat the oven to 140°C (275°F/Gas 1). Split the vanilla bean lengthways and scrape out the seeds, then combine the bean and seeds with the milk in a saucepan. Bring the milk just to the boil.

Meanwhile, whisk together the egg yolks, egg and sugar in a bowl until well combined. Strain the milk over the egg mixture and stir to combine. Skim the surface to remove any foam.

Ladle the mixture into four 125 ml (4 fl oz/¹/2 cup) ramekins and place in a roasting tin. Pour enough hot water into the tin to come halfway up the sides of the ramekins. Bake for 30 minutes, or until just firm to the touch. Transfer the ramekins to a wire rack to cool, then refrigerate until ready to serve.

CARAMEL SQUARES

MAKES 15 SQUARES

185 g (6 $^1/_2$ oz/1 $^1/_2$ cups) plain (all-purpose) flour
1 $^1/_2$ tablespoons caster (superfine) sugar
100 g (3 $^1/_2$ oz) butter, chopped
1 egg

CARAMEL
400 g (14 oz) tin sweetened condensed milk
20 g ($^3/_4$ oz) butter
1 tablespoon golden syrup, dark corn syrup or treacle

CHOCOLATE TOPPING
120 g (4 $^1/_4$ oz) dark chocolate, chopped
40 g (1 $^1/_2$ oz) butter

METHOD Brush a 17 x 26 cm (6 $^1/_2$ x 10 $^1/_2$ inch) shallow
rectangular tin with melted butter and then line the base with
baking paper.

Combine the flour and sugar in a bowl, then add the butter.
Using your fingertips, rub the butter in until the mixture

resembles breadcrumbs. Stir in the egg and enough water to form a coarse dough, then press the dough together on a lightly floured surface. Wrap the dough in plastic wrap and refrigerate for 30 minutes, or until firm.

Preheat the oven to 210ºC (415ºF/Gas 6–7). Roll out the pastry between two pieces of baking paper to fit the base of the tin. Cover the pastry in the tin with baking paper, fill with baking beads, dried beans or rice, then bake for 10 minutes. Remove the beads and paper, then bake for another 10 minutes or until golden. Remove from the oven. Reduce the oven to 180ºC (350ºF/Gas 4).

To make the caramel, combine all the ingredients in a small saucepan. Stir over medium–low heat until the butter melts and the mixture boils and thickens. Spread in a thin layer over the pastry and bake for 10 minutes, or until firm. Allow to cool.

To make the topping, combine the chocolate and butter in a bowl set over a saucepan of simmering water. Stir the mixture until melted and well combined, allow to cool slightly, then pour over the caramel. Leave to set, then cut into squares.

The squares will keep, stored in an airtight container in a cool, dark place, for 2 days.

PINEAPPLE & SOUR CREAM GRATIN

SERVES 4

800 g (1 lb 12 oz) ripe pineapple, cut into 1.5 cm
($^5/_8$ inch) pieces
60 ml (2 fl oz/$^1/_4$ cup) dark rum
45 g (1$^1/_2$ oz) unsalted butter
1 teaspoon natural vanilla extract
$^1/_2$ teaspoon ground ginger
140 g (5 oz/$^3/_4$ cup lightly packed) soft brown sugar
300 g (10$^1/_2$ oz/1$^1/_4$ cups) sour cream or quark
60 ml (2 fl oz/$^1/_4$ cup) cream
1 teaspoon finely grated lemon zest

METHOD   Preheat an oven grill (broiler) to medium–high.

Combine the pineapple, rum, butter, vanilla extract, ginger
and $^1/_4$ cup of the sugar in a large saucepan. Cook, stirring
occasionally, over medium–high heat for 8–10 minutes, or until
the sugar has dissolved and the mixture is very reduced and
caramelised. Remove from the heat, divide the mixture among
four individual gratin dishes and allow to cool slightly.

Combine the sour cream or quark, cream and lemon zest in a bowl and whisk until smooth. Divide the mixture among the dishes, smoothing the tops.

Sprinkle the remaining brown sugar over the top of the sour cream mixture, then cook under the grill for 4–5 minutes, or until the sugar has caramelised, taking care not to burn the sugar. Serve immediately.

CANNOLI

MAKES 12

FILLING
500 g (1 lb 2 oz/2 cups) ricotta cheese (see Note, page 74)
1/4 teaspoon orangeflower water
100 g (3 1/2 oz/ 1/2 cup) cedro, diced (see Notes)
60 g (2 1/4 oz) bittersweet chocolate, coarsely grated
1 tablespoon grated orange zest
60 g (2 1/4 oz/1/2 cup) icing (confectioners') sugar

DOUGH
300 g (10 1/2 oz/2 1/3 cups) plain (all-purpose) flour
1 tablespoon caster (superfine) sugar
1/2 teaspoon ground cinnamon
40 g (1 1/2 oz) unsalted butter
60 ml (2 fl oz/1/4 cup) sweet Marsala
vegetable oil, for deep-frying
icing (confectioners') sugar, for dusting

METHOD To make the filling, combine all the ingredients in
a bowl and mix to combine well. Cover with plastic wrap and
refrigerate while you prepare the dough.

To make the dough, combine the flour, sugar and cinnamon in a bowl, rub in the butter and add the Marsala. Mix until the dough comes together in a loose clump, then knead on a lightly floured surface for 4–5 minutes, or until smooth. Wrap in plastic wrap and refrigerate for at least 30 minutes.

Cut the dough in half and roll each piece out on a lightly floured surface into a sheet about 5 mm (¼ inch) thick. Cut each dough half into six 9 cm (3½ inch) squares. Place a metal cannoli tube (see Notes) diagonally across the middle of each square. Fold the sides over the tube, moistening the overlap with water, then press together to seal.

Fill a large deep frying pan one-third full of oil and heat it to 180°C (350°F), or until a cube of bread dropped into the pan browns in 15 seconds. Drop one or two tubes at a time into the hot oil. Fry until golden brown and crisp. Remove from the oil. Gently remove the moulds and drain on crumpled paper towels. When the pastry shells are cool, fill a piping (icing) bag with the ricotta mixture and fill the shells. Serve dusted with icing sugar.

NOTES Cedro, also known as citron, is a citrus fruit with a very thick, knobbly skin that is used to make candied peel. Cannoli tubes are available at kitchenware shops.

NEW YORK CHEESECAKE

SERVES 8–10

PASTRY

60 g (4 oz/^{1}/$_2$ cup) self-raising flour

230 g (8 oz/1^3/$_4$ cups) plain (all-purpose) flour

60 g (2^1/$_4$ oz/^{1}/$_4$ cup) caster (superfine) sugar

1 teaspoon finely grated lemon zest

80 g (2^3/$_4$ oz) butter

2 eggs, lightly beaten

FILLING

750 g (1 lb 10 oz/3 cups) curd cheese or
   cream cheese, softened

230 g (8 oz/1 cup) caster (superfine) sugar

60 g (2^1/$_4$ oz/^{1}/$_2$ cup) plain (all-purpose) flour

2 teaspoons grated orange zest

2 teaspoons grated lemon zest

4 eggs

170 ml (5^1/$_2$ fl oz/^{2}/$_3$ cup) cream

glacé (candied) citrus slices, to decorate (optional;
   see Note)

METHOD Combine the flours, sugar and lemon zest in a bowl. Add the butter and then, using your fingertips, rub in until the mixture resembles coarse breadcrumbs. Add the egg and mix well. Gradually add 3–4 tablespoons cold water to give a coarse dough, then turn out onto a lightly floured surface and gather into a ball. Wrap in plastic wrap and refrigerate for 20 minutes.

Preheat the oven to 210°C (415°F/Gas 6–7). Roll the pastry out between two sheets of baking paper to line a greased 22 cm (8 inch) round springform cake tin, then trim the edges. Cover the pastry with baking paper, fill with baking beads, dried beans or rice, then bake for 10 minutes. Remove the paper and beads and bake for a further 5 minutes or until light golden. Allow to cool. Reduce the oven to 150°C (300°F/Gas 2).

To make the filling, beat the cream cheese, sugar, flour and zests with electric beaters until smooth. Add the eggs, one at a time, beating well after each addition. Stir in the cream, then pour over the pastry. Bake for 1 hour 25 minutes, or until almost set. Cool in the oven, then chill until firm. Serve decorated with glacé citrus slices, if desired.

NOTE Glacé (candied) citrus slices are available from delicatessens and speciality food stores.

Published in 2009 by Murdoch Books Pty Limited

Murdoch Books Australia
Pier 8/9
23 Hickson Road
Millers Point NSW 2000
Phone: +61 (0) 2 8220 2000
Fax: +61 (0) 2 8220 2558
www.murdochbooks.com.au

Murdoch Books UK Limited
Erico House, 6th Floor
93–99 Upper Richmond Road
Putney, London SW15 2TG
Phone: +44 (0) 20 8785 5995
Fax: +44 (0) 20 8785 5985
www.murdochbooks.co.uk

Chief Executive: Juliet Rogers
Commissioning Editor: Lynn Lewis
Senior Designer: Heather Menzies
Series Designer: Jacqueline Richards
Project Manager: Justine Harding
Production: Alexandra Gonzalez
Photographer: George Seper
Stylist: Marie-Hélène Clauzon

National Library of Australia Cataloguing-in-Publication Data
Author: Kitchen, Leanne
Title: Recipes from the Dairy / Leanne Kitchen.
ISBN: 9781741964288 (pbk.)
Series: Mini Providore. Notes: Includes index.
Subjects: Cookery (Dairy products) Dairy products.
Dewey Number: 641.67

Printed by 1010 Printing International Limited in 2009. PRINTED IN CHINA.